Quiet Storm

A Collection of Poetry

A Flower
To Soften
The Hour
© 2006 H. Storm

by Hélène Storm

To Dear Rosa —

If only... if I could speak...

with "Words" I cannot find,
"The Words" you'd understand, I'm sure.

With Love & "The Best" of
Wishes for "The Best"

Hélène Storm

CELEBRITY PRESS INCORPORATED, PUBLISHERS • LOS ANGELES

10th day of September, 2006

QUIET STORM
Published By
Celebrity Press Incorporated
Los Angeles, California

Copyright © 1981 Helene Storm
First Printing, November 1981

ISBN: 0-9607412-0-8
Library of Congress Catalogue Card No. 81-70299

*Soon to be available in cassette recitations
by the author. Inquiries should be addressed to:*

Celebrity Press Incorporated
Post Office Box 48-896A
Los Angeles, California 90048

Cover Photographs By: ▆▆ Storm
Cover Designed By: Richard DeSiato

Printed in the United States of America

Helene Storm

November 1, 1981

Dear Reader —

It is my purpose in these pages to capture the intensity of life.

I do hope you feel the warmth and share the strength of understanding: So far to reach, so much to know —

My love extends to you — And I thank you for finding yourself with me in these pages —

Helene Storm

CONTENTS

PREFACE . . .

I BELIEVE THE BEGINNING

IS A QUIET STORM.

I BELIEVE

I Believe . . . That simple, is not a complex thing.
I Believe . . . Complexity stems from within.

I Believe . . . In the unbelievable, and what I think is not.
I Believe . . . In realizing what we have, but yet quite haven't got.

I Believe . . . That love is born in "every" form of art.
I Believe . . . That Man and science are sculptured from the heart.

I Believe . . . In you, as you are made of time.
And I Believe we live . . .
            As a carefully pointed rhyme.
            We've made our way to know,
            Beyond a dashing start . . .
                And I Believe
                I Believe you know what I mean.

I Believe in it all,
And I Believe in more.
I Believe it's all attached . . .
                The ceiling and the floor.
I Believe there is no way
That isn't at our door.

So I Believe,
As I Believe it's true,
It's only 'round the corner . . .
What you see as new.

I Believe it's the sky or the ocean . . .
That you thought you knew before,
Until you saw it suddenly
        And you knew you believed in more.

It lives in you who walks away
And lives in you who stays,
It reaches out in every form
That finds another way.

So I Believe in it all,
And I Believe in you.
I Believe it's all
Like in the spinning of a dime,
I Believe we spend only a moment's time.

I Believe our feet
Walk higher than the floor
I Believe . . .
        And I Believe in more.

THE BEGINNING

Think not too long in this listening, My Friend:

Life is the finding of a little square in a long, narrow tunnel.

The love one knows exists is found somehow in thought
In the profile of the smile that looks to another spot.

To know the green of colors and the blue of skies
And the living carvings of Life's surmise.

To capture a word etched with an inkless pen
That speaks in that moment of a beginning that it sends.

O' Poetry, you are my reflection of the carvings of the pen —
The music that begins in sounds that never end.

My ears are the vessels of an etched heart
That struggles to find the way to a start.

I find the day has found me again
As time gives the hours a place to spend.

"QUIET STORM"

I've idealized my ways a bit
To see how things should surely fit.

Reality is a skinny thought
That sometimes leaves you in a knot.
You twist and turn until you learn
And then you've earned so much.

But somehow things will "always be"
The silence in their mystery.

I am this "Quiet Storm" who has touched
The beginnings of many thoughts.

This "Quiet Storm" who longs for warmth:
Who looks for the rhyme in all that I find.

HARD TO FORGET...

HARD TO SEE

THE HARD TO FIND,

HARD TO LOSE YOU

FROM MY MIND

DO YOU KNOW THE FEELING?

The night's up again . . .

And so am I; wish I could sleep.

"IT'S OVER"

What do you say

    When it's dark outside

        And you know the morning's almost here?

When you stop to think

        Your tired eyes still wonder when

        Officially these moments end;

And then . . .

    What do you say? . . .

When you know the morning's atmosphere

    And thinking won't make it disappear;

When the darkness slides to the other side

    And the light is all too clear to revenge

    A sudden dawning end,

    What do you say? . . .

        "IT'S OVER"

I'VE LEFT YOU THERE

It's been a long time . . .
I've left you by yourself

My thoughts are mine,
And without you, for a change.

The books I've read
Were meant for me
And time sees much too clearly
How I've changed in attitude and understanding

It's been a long time . . .
I've left you by yourself
Since I've stopped to recognize
The precision in your sweetness
And the careful aggression of your madness

But all around me,
It's still there
Just as you once were
In my prayers.

But it's been too long
To dream you care . . .

I'VE LEFT YOU THERE.

HOW I FANTASIZED

I fantasized him to be
The answer, my ideal.

Whether right, or wrong,
His image, it remains,
And does retain a crazy focus.

Misjudged notions . . .
Touched off tokens . . .
Lost emotions . . .

> Beyond the feeling of any sense of pain,
> The actions are the game
> That let me take my careful aim.

"P.S." I Love You . . .

> For your thoughts
> That did get lost
> In all the ways we did
>
> And your simple complex face
> That did exist to be my hiding place
>
> In your eyes, I saw my face
> And I somehow knew it was misplaced
> Because I loved you for the thoughts
> That lived in you as the existence
> Of a discovery.

"P.S." I Love You . . .

> *For the atmosphere*
> *We found together*
> *That held me long enough*
> *So I could begin to battle*
> *That which enslaved me.*
>
> *And I love you still*
> *Because of questions*
> *We did spill.*
>
> *Questions that never sank*
> *With the moment, even though*
> *The beauty of our presence was so strong.*
>
> *I love you still,*
> *Because the answers*
> *Will always be a part of you.*

IT WAS MORE THAN ONE COULD SAY

Further away
Than the average day
It was there
Where we played . . .

It was love
Or it was play,
But it was more than one could say.

Until you found that it was,
You did not know you knew.

It was somehow . . .
That we found the way
And some way
That there was the time . . .

The time was more
Than one could say.

It was love,
Or it was play,
But it was
More than one could say.

MOMENTS

The days that I've touched with you, Dear
Have all turned to be mirrors
Of the moments in time
That could never go by
Without knowing that I've . . .

Lived . . .
In your heart and your arms
I've found smiles in your eyes,
And I've kissed you good-bye.

> *In moments . . .*
> *That could never be spoken*
> *Live the words of a lifetime*
> *That will always be there*
> *For the moments are rare*
> *When you've found in your mind*
> *Things you will sing for all time.*

THE SKIER

The skier that I know was born yesterday,
And today he skis.

I remember him as Life's skier
Who wanted to be free to jump off the mountain
Wishing evryone well —

But the skier who'd dare not leave
Permanent tracts:

> So, he could climb the mountain, and breathe the air
> And be as free as only he would let himself be.

I never got to ski the mountain,
But somehow I know we shared the view.

I realized had I gotten close, I would melt
His polar ice caps and his ego would lose
Its refrigeration:

> So, all things happen for the best
> And his ego can maintain itself.

THE IMPRESSION

The quickness of the tap

The looking for the rap

The finding that the touch,

> *However slight,*

Leaves its impression.

"THE LION AND THE FISH"

The roar of the lion
Was an easy-going man.

He made it easy to relax in quiet laughter,
And made me know the joy of having fun.

The sensitivity of the fish
Made him a hard person to touch.

He made it easy for me to think "good-bye."
He swam in isolated waters and kept a tight ship.

The heart of the lion was generous to all.

The tail of the fish always kept himself moving forward
With his very smooth strokes.

No one would dare to stay too long with the lion,
As restless as they are,

                    And

No one would dare to share the waters of
The ever-growing fish!

IN A MEMORY

*Everything on Earth
Has been written about,
In a memory.*

*Both the sky
And the sea
And the ocean breeze,
Of a memory.*

*I see now
That they all just belong to the sky . . .
The sky finding earth,
To the rainbows hitting dirt,
To the mountains
And the sea
And the birds living in the trees
That live within me in today
And tell me
It's okay,
There's no memory to pay,
But life only today.*

*Live the moment that is
And never kiss from afar,
Just let go
That falling star,
Of a memory.*

ANXIETY

I don't want the pain
Of things not sustained.

Anxiety will pull itself through again.

I've searched for you
In corridors of Time.
I've brought you back to moments found.

The vision was truly
More the pleasure,
The intrigue, the sin.

MIRAGES OF YOU

Crying skies will dry to shine . . .

> *Mirages of you.*

Nature's loving touch
> *On molded rock*
> > *That listened so well*
> > > *To the pounding surf,*

Has found today's "Hello"
> *In winds that blow* . . .

> > *MIRAGES OF YOU.*

I REMEMBER

It is the infinitesimal pleasures of Life

That strive to survive the vintage of Time.

It is the delight

In the moment that lets go

That I care to remember.

FOR ME:

He has the power to create
Yet he won't let himself be bait.

He could be just the reason why
That I choose to verbalize.

I wonder when I can pretend
That I have more than just a friend.

It is too much for me to ask
That he allow me to be glad.

He's good to me from time-to-time
And this allows the sublime to shine.

With love to you my parting friend,
It's a shame this poem, too, must end.

I WONDER

I Wonder about the wood and the rock

I Wonder about the breeze and the trees

I Wonder about the birds and the bees

I Wonder about the love that I leave.

I Wonder about the sky in the night

I Wonder about the dreams that I fight

I Wonder about the day that will come

I Wonder about the things love has done.

I Wonder about the quiet in the air

I Wonder about the thoughts that are there

I Wonder about the ways that I dare

I Wonder about you over there . . .

I WONDER.

GRAINS IN MEMORY LANE

The grain of the wood draws a picture
Of the wooden knots that must remain
The things that cannot change
The circles in a frame.

We are not to blame
That we are not the same
Our windowpane is grained
And it can never change

Quietly we go
As the melting snow
Moments melt time away
Love builds what stays

Lingering streets in our mind
Memories of days we can't find
Quietly leaving my thoughts
Quietly finding the knots

Circles of grains in a frame
Pictures of wood that remain
Quietly melting away
Quietly finding what stays

Wishing you were here
To see views disappear
Touching them one more time
Leaving the days far behind

Images in my mind
Pictures left of time
Quietly will go
As the melting snow

Pictures that remain
Circles of the grain
Moments in a frame
Forever we remain.

10,000 FEET OF SNOW

I let go

10,000 feet of snow

A love that wouldn't grow.

This forest, it remains

In icicles it's framed.

THE SEARCH . . .

I FIND YOU

EVERYWHERE,

MY LOVE,

THAT MY HEART LOOKS

YOU'LL BE THERE

Here and there

I'll find you:

> *Beyond the desk that holds your thought*

> *Behind the light that lets me see*

> *In books I've lifted to be free*

> *Together we — just you and me.*

> *In pictures far and close at hand*

> *We are the thoughts, we understand.*

FIRST DATE

We were captured:

    Threads of perception,

        Intertwined . . .

Intertwined words of time,

    Embraced with understanding.

We were captured

    Sharing space

        Words apart, and to themselves,

And, now,

    Together,

        It's okay.

THE GREAT ESCAPE

Can one believe the touch of a caress

That feels so good against my chest?

People say that it must be —

So you can know the feeling of humanity.

Humanity will walk in perfect fitted shoes

From here to there and everywhere

And know not where they have been.

The great escape is what they want,

And they are all lost in the search of it.

TO FIND

To find the love

To share the dreams

That one lives,

The strength to search

Must be as great

As the dreams that fill your heart.

The fire of Life is lit

When the match is struck.

1:13 A.M.

Wish I could write
With words I can't find.

Please, Please . . . if only I could explain,
The words you'd understand, I'm sure.

But they're lost in twisted things to say,
Lost forever in today.

I'm lost too, you know,
Finding everything much too slow.

It's such a slow road to walk,
It's such a hard road to talk.

I hope and hope for what's ahead,
I dream of wishes that are dead.

But I'm alive, and so is time,
I'll find quiet survival to be my rival.
Sleep is near, I'll find you here.

AND EVEN THOUGH . . .

And even though
My heart has felt
The bits of time
Moments crossing in line
The deepest touch
To touch me yet.

Wide open eyes
Still searching time

And even though
I'm tough, you know
I cry a lot
In many spots.

And even though
I live my time
I'll always know
That you were mine.

And even though
We've never met
Somehow I'll know
I'll not forget
My feelings deep
That search for you.

And even though
Life lives, you know,
My feelings thrive
In hopes you
Will arrive.

M U S I C

Music fills the air with perfumes yet not discovered

How lovely it would be to smell that note so sharp

And that flat so provoking!

THE DESERT

Before the having,
And first the wanting,
Lives a field of growth.

It does seem to be a desert
When you search for what you have not.

I'm such a big space
Compared to the two who share mistakes.

Memories live in moments
That enlarge as time moves on.

The slightest touch
Resounds in a million melodies.

THE ABSTRACT

In constant vigilance of the minutes in the hour,

I live and breathe:

> The sky is blue
> The sky is dark
> One day following the next.

The abstract of nature is so real it touches you,

And for the moment you can forget your purpose,

The reason for which you know you must exist:

> The questions that you must know and answer.

And in this search, one does accept oneself as being

The only solid object in a spinning world.

He touched me with his look, and warmed me with his touch.

We shared, and he thought he knew me.

It wasn't much, for the feelings in my eyes were never spoken

And could never be explained.

He came and went, and never knew the view.

The world spins on, and we have shared a minute or two

In the hours of our years, and I will remember him as I

Remember all of the abstract in my world,

For he has changed it but a bit.

MEANING

Oh so deep

And oh so hard to find

When searching on your own

And finding your thoughts alone:

> *Life's meaning makes its mark,*

> *But never exists to find*

> *The reality of its meaning.*

PAINS OF PASSION

So wild am I,

I wish I could die

To be saved from suffering

Pains of passion.

The mission of the heart is

An explosive journey through

The battlefields of Life.

HOW LONG?

How long?

Is not long:

It's just a matter of time.

When time does
Give a result you'll see

You need not count
From whence it be

Forever and a day
Is too long to pray

From day-to-day
Along the way

The time will pay
The finding day.

THE SEARCH

More than an echo
More than a song
More than the wind
That always plays along

More than the river
More than the sea
More than the mountains
Do I look for thee

I find you everywhere, My Love,
That my heart looks.

REVELATION

To understand and to know,
One must seek.

With open eyes
And an open heart,
There are many answers to be found.

There are none so blinded
By the light of truth —
Whatever truth it be,
Than those who can, but will not see.

DREAMS OF DEVOTION . . .

WE ALL LOOK TO FIND

WHAT WE SEE

IN ONE ANOTHER'S MIND

BREAKFAST

It was morning

And we were new

There was coffee —

Me and You

In the distance

Of all others

Softly smiling

To each other . . .

Have a biscuit,
Taste the honey,

Loves a moment
That stops running!

REFLECTION OF A MAN

In arms so sensitive and strong
He held humor's wit and man's devine desire.

Deliberation kissed his mean upper lip,
As he said nothing.

I liked him for his way of making it all seem
Okay.

I fell for his passive-aggressive mental stage.

That night's dream
Was that we were a team.

THE CHANCE

Maybe the magic will go away

Or can we take the chance

That it will stay?

Some day when there are no more

Words to say,

Maybe the magic will go away.

THE MAN I'LL LOVE

For him to love the love in me

For him to see the depths I see

For him to hold me ever fast

The man whose look will ever last.

The man whose touch will always be,

For he will be the treasure

Locked in a heart of gold,

For he will hold the only key

To make my dreams unfold.

"FOREVER YOU, FOREVER ME"

Out of today
Has passed a night
Out of the night
Has come a light
You are my days
You are my nights
There is no darkness.

> *Forever you and forever me*
> *Living time and eternity*
> *Our love is strong and our hearts are one*
> *The love of two is one.*

We've found the reasons
We are meant to be
We feel our dreams
As we set them free
To Life's embrace
And constant stare
We touch, love is there.

> *Forever you and forever me*
> *Living time and eternity*
> *Our love is strong and our hearts are one*
> *The love of two is one.*

We live today
Far beyond our time
And in love's silence
We hear the sound
Creating time
That always will be.

Forever you and forever me
Living time and eternity
Our love is strong and our hearts are one
The love of two is one.

A strength like ours shines
For all eyes to see
The world goes 'round
Finding you touching me
As night slips into
The coming day,
It sings out to say:

Forever you and forever me
Living time and eternity
Our love is strong and our hearts are one
The love of two is one.

THE TASTE

Bring me an apple

So I can taste the pear.

Bring me an orange

And I will know the lime.

Bring me your heart

And I will find your soul.

Let me live in your arms

As we taste of control.

MELODY IN THE NIGHT

I wait for the melody of tonight
In a room we've built to be our Life.
We'll dance the night into the day:
We'll live the moments we've been away.

A bit of you, a taste of me.
A tab that pulls a string that sings
The knob that's turned for an open door
My hunger pangs in taste for more.

A bit of you, a taste of me.
And so it is with harmony
Melodies of you in times of me
In echoes of all things that be.

You need the touch of my caress
To grow the love that we possess;
The softest touch of you and me
The elegance of we so free.

Seasonings of you in tastes of me
In quiet traveling melodies.

Just take my arm and kiss my neck
I can begin to breathe your breath.
Melodies of you in times of me
And so it is with harmony.

LOVE

To see   *Is to want*

To want   *Is to feel*

To feel   *Is to touch*

To touch   *Is to hold*

To hold   *Is to keep*

To keep   *Is to treasure*

To treasure *Is to have and to hold forever.*

THE TOUCH

You need the touch of my caress

To let you feel the person that you are.

Together we "are" the beauty in each other:

Apart we are but an image.

ALONG YOUR WAY

I hold you in the night
Your arms caress me tight

Loving you, as I do
Here I stay, along your way

You sigh a soft caress
My breasts upon your chest

I lay with you
Play with you
Be with you
Talk to you

As I do, loving you
Along your way

For all I do with you
Are dreams that all come true

Just loving you, as I do
Along your way

To breathe with you, my pet,
And know that we have met

Along your way, the other day
Loving you, as I do

Born for you, to share with you
Who's to say this was not meant to be
A real fantasy?

I hold you in the night:
Your arms caress me tight.

THE BALANCE OF NATURE

The morning has not quite awakened, but so many mornings
Have past which were not spoken for.

Though you have chosen to be where you are, My Love,
And not here with me —

> As your working mind prevails;
> As my loving soul prevails,

I find you here with me this morning, as in mornings past,

> As you've reached for me
> As I reached for you
> In just the moment past.

The shadows of the slow-moving leaves
Upon my windows' drapes
Speak of the balance of nature
After the howling wind has ceased.

A peaceful balance of Life's stormy nature
That you and I will find in the eyes and arms of each other.

NOW THAT I'VE FOUND YOU

Somewhere there was you
Before I knew you

Somewhere there was time
That existed without you

But you were around
When I least expected,
Inside my mind
It was you I detected

I'm so happy for it all
Now that I've found you,
After all.

THE WORLD

The world was built for us to share
As Man was created to breathe the air.

We'll live each other's night and day
We'll work and play as we feel we may.

We'll breathe the air that we will share
We'll live to know that "We" are there.

I'll be you and
You'll be me,
And still there will be some mystery.

We'll know that all the things that ever lived
Were made for us before we were kids.

We'll live the priceless time we share
Always knowing the value of having each other there.

TORCH OF LIFE

I want to be the light in the flame of your Life.

Together we must be the torch of understanding

And radiate the liberty we both share.

WHISPERINGS

Here we stand on the sand of this traveling land

Whispering, hand-in-hand, all the secrets of Man

I love you, you love me

We are whispering trees

Whisperings whispering in the air dreams that we share.

Hand-in-hand where we stand on this traveling sand

You touch me, I touch you
As we cling to the land

Whisperings whispering kisses of thoughts

Whisperings whispering what lovers have got.

My sweet love we are here for the moment we stand

Take my hand, can you hear all the whispering sands?

    Don't let go,

    It's not time for the end

Take my hand with the wind, let me hear it again.

Whisperings whispering moments we spend

    I love you, you love me

    We are whispering trees

Live the breeze in the leaves in the time that we seize

As we stand on the sand

    Hand-in-hand.

RHYTHM

In rhythm

Do I feel for you, Dear

With the beats of my heart

And the ticks of the clock

I know that the music we make

Creates sounds never played,

Creates Life never portrayed.

YOU ARE:

The warmth
The day
The moment's say

The heart
The start
The loving part

The sigh
The eye
That kisses mine

The slow
The rushing
Of the time

The just
The lust
That leads to trust

The wish
The thought
The moving sought

The toy
The game
The perfect aim

The model
The teacher
That makes it easy

You are
You see, the one for me.

MARRIAGE

Two people together

Forming their own country,

With the world as their boundary.

THE PARENTS' WISH

The nights are long
The days are warm
We make a wish for the child that's born.

A child of strength as the tallest tree
A child as bright as the stars can be.

He'll be the sun for all to see
He'll be the brightness of his mom and daddy.
The love they share will shine through him:
The smiles, the thoughts, the crazy whims.

We'll share the days that he'll begin.
We'll learn from him as we watch him grow
And remember things we have let go.

And, so, from two there will be three:
       Three very lucky children.

MY LITTLE BEETHOVEN

We could be the colors in the rainbow
And the whiteness of the snow
I could be the violin
And you, the bow.

My Little Beethoven,
You bear the beauty of the music in the field
In a chest that won't let anybody know
It breathes and feels.

Before the night has found its spinning wheel,
More than you realize in the seriousness of
Your brow, in yesterday's beginning
A symphony we found.

The sounds of love through the changing moons
And a little bit of sun thrown in my room.

Living the darkness in the light of love,
The symphony we feel will know that it was
Real:

> Sounds have a way of knowing the tune
> Before the "key" in the music can be
> Construed.

WAS IT LOVE?

Was it Monday
You stayed?
        Was it Tuesday
        You stayed away?
          It was Wednesday
          When it rained all day.
            Thursday, when you were
            So far away.

Was it love? . . . Making things too hard to say?
Was it love? . . . Making you stay away?
Was it love? . . . Killing me day-by-day?
Was it love? . . . Feeling that way?

Now it's Friday
I relive words you said
        Saturday makes me
        Feel afraid
          Until Sunday,
          When you will phone
            And suddenly "I"
            Was never alone.

(see next page)

Was it love? . . . Making things too hard to say?
Was it love? . . . Making you stay away?
Was it love? . . . Killing me day-by-day?
Was it love? . . . Feeling that way?

Bringing you, in my heart
Making days, never part
Living you, from the start:
Letting me be, in your heart.

Was it me
Was it you
Was it me?
    Was it love
    That the time
    Could not see?
        Was it me
        Was it you
        Was it me?
            Was it true
            What we found
            Could it be?
                Now the time
                Stays behind
                When you were mine.

I DREAMED

I dreamed
Too long
Of what I felt,

But was it wrong
To make a dream
Become more than what it meant?

It's just a dream,
You see —
I know it's not reality.

"But, what is reality, anyway?"
But a sight reaching out so right
That it could possibly exist
Long enough to say ... "IT'S THERE."

MISUNDERSTANDING...

SO MANY PERFECT

MISUNDERSTANDINGS

WE KNOW EACH OTHER WELL ENOUGH . . .

We know
Each other
Well enough
To say "Good-Bye."

Before . . .
I was curious about you.

And I would love that gleaming "I"
That I'd become when you'd come by

I would see you
Through your ways of
Twisted tries and alibis

Just wouldn't care
As long as we did still share

Oh tenderly you left my heart
With strokes above and far apart
I grew from you and saw the dark
Of shades that shadowed your swift art.

Your strokes no longer find the way
I see the games your touchdowns play.

*You smile away
And say it's sad
That we somehow
Cannot be glad*

*So I give way to
Say "Good-bye"
To such a curiously,
Funny "Hi"*

*I now know the "vibes" of you
Are always tried,
But left untrue*

*Your strokes are a joke
And your face is a hoax*

We know each other well enough

To say "Good-Bye."

ONCE UPON A TIME

Once upon a time . . .

He said, "So tell me about yourself,"

And I paused . . . and said: "I'm for real."

And he said: "What?"

And then I thought how unexplainably

Phony that seemed for me to say —

Until . . . I realized he wasn't quite
for real, not really,

And I could then more easily explain what I meant . . .

At least to myself.

SOUND MEETING SILENCE

So many times

In so many ways

The moments of sound

Have created the silence.

I speak to you silence

As only you can understand:

How reality creates the deafness,

And how love is the ultimate silence . . .

As the blooming fruit of the quiet tree!

MISUNDERSTANDING

If only you would know
Your love doesn't have to grow
You would be more kind to me
If only you would know.

If only you would see
How I want you so
And how my heart could find the key . . .

But . . .
        You've done me in today
        You've hurt me in your way
        You've stopped the very chance
        Of living in romance

        And I'm tortured by your ways,
        They sharpen all my pains.
        But it's hard for me to say . . .
        "I'm leaving you today."

If only you had known
Your love didn't have to grow
You could have been more kind
If only you had known.

If only you had known
My heart could not let go,
You were the one it had to know . . .

> *Babe, you never would've gone*
> *On hurting me this way . . .*
> *Or looked into my eyes*
> *When you smiled your funny lies,*
> *You might have looked to see*
> *How, together, we were free,*
> *And, how it was love . . . for me.*

If only you had known
The words were there for you to say,
I would have stayed and been your friend,
And, maybe, loved you to the end.

THAT'S THE WAY IT GOES!

He could care more
He could care less,
Nothing interfers with his happiness.

Nothing seems to bother the righteousness of him
When righteousness was only made to meet his every whim.

He promises, nor does he do
A thing along the way,
For nothing should intrude the view
He sees beyond his nose today.

He can only be the victory
And never have the pleasure of a contradictory.

His high regard for all he sees that he dare speak about
Is worth the value of an echo in an empty canyon.

To think
I've loved with such a man
Makes me wonder who I am.

To fall in love with such a man
Makes me see the sap I am.

SENTIMENTAL LOVE

If one

Can only look above

A sentimental love,

Then one can look to find

What remains behind.

I never knew you,

Until I realized

I didn't love you.

A DINNER DATE THAT LOST AN APPETITE

Suddenly I couldn't chew a word

I thought I was a dentist

Because words were so lost in his thoughts

All I could see were teeth.

We never made it to the restaurant "Pot Luck"

Because "Pot Luck" was not good enough:

Better luck next time . . .

Good-Bye Forever.

TASTELESS LOVERS

The lives of many tasteless lovers —

Forever reaching out and touching the emptiness

Of a dark-filled room:

>*Only to dream, but never to taste*

>*The richness of a love that lasts forever.*

TO HIM

He stands so straight

As he looks so softly

At all that he perceives.

I love him so

But he doesn't know

In my heart he could never be replaced!

TOUCH ME A THING TO SAY

Don't point
Your finger to my chest

Don't point
At me 'cause I'm the best

You've had your chance to dance along
Dance to the music that's my song.

You've left today
You've gone away
And I —
I'm not the same

I feel the blame
Of you and I,
I feel the song
That has just died.

Fly away
With me
Let it seem
To be

Sing me
Away today
Touch me a thing to say.

ANOTHER WAY

Would I be right?
Would I be wrong?
Or would it be just another way?

I spoke too soon
To my father today
Only because I wanted
To make him see my say

I doubt that he'll remember
The words,
Other than
The new and other way
I appeared to him today

He'll remember me
In another way
After today!

GOLD

Gold is cold

And luck

Does not come

With the pot.

IDENTITY...

AN EMOTIONAL CORNERSTONE

THAT LIVES IN THE CROSS-FIRE

OF SELF-EVALUATION

MAN VERSUS WOMAN

We look for the strength

Of each other's warmth,

Only to find:

The strength of the other is our weakness.

TOO MANY WORDS

Will it be your questioning that finds the answer?

Will it be your searching that finds the truth?

Will it be the waiting that finds a moment?

Or will it be the moment that loses itself tonight?

Can two be together when the distance is unknown?

Can forever live the emptiness alone?

Can the task be easy when the competition is so strong?

Can the challenge be less complex

       That success will know its home?

SUSPENDED SENSE OF REALITY

Sometimes, what you're trying to change

Makes all the difference in the world:

Sometimes, it doesn't matter!

THE APPEARANCE

Nobody knows
The inner turmoil
That creates the outer being . . .

It's just a single wonder
That fights to persist
In a reason to exist.

Nobody knows
The reality that
Hides from reasons to appear.

I'm hiding, I'm hiding,
I don't want the world to see me here.

Question your friend,
Only to be scared away . . .
His appearance is not
Where he is today.

Don't look away,
Because "the distance" won't
It's just where it stays.

And nobody knows
The inner turmoil
That creates the outer being.

PHILOSOPHY

We are born by chance,
Or so it is said.

Do we dare live by chance,
Or make the effort to dream ahead?

We live for today,
In hopes for tomorrow.

Dream in the night of wonders in our day,
And think in the day of the enchantment of the night.

Where do we go
From where we have been?

Do we attempt to decide?
When decisions choose their own narrow path
And create their own narrow choice.

Am I here to live?
Live in short-lived choices?

Or am I here to look in all directions?

> I Look . . .
> I See . . .
> I Wonder . . .

Should I look to find
Or just look to see?

I once thought I knew,
For I thought I knew you
And I thought I knew me

At this moment, the sea is calm
I dare not look at the horizon:

2:09 a.m. — Too early to be the morning;
              Too late to be the night.

WHO WE ARE!

It is the way you bite the apple
That feeds your very soul

It is your method of combustion
That becomes the way you go.

There are many ways to split an apple
There are many ways to cut the cake

There are many ways that we can look up
There are many ways we can find fate.

Though the roads are many,
Our decisions are few
Because our points of travel
Are carefully selected by our views.

You can't begin a roadmap
Without knowing where to go
So you look around and find
The yes's and the no's.

It's a slender road that travels
To where it is you go
It's only your decisions
That begin to tell you so.

That's why, you see, some people travel
To distant remote points,
While others, they remain,
Not far beyond their boat.

It is the will
That pulls the chains
That drives us all
Or makes us lame.

OUR FELLOWMAN

I sometimes wonder of the restless bird I am
In my searching and questioning my fellowman.

I look at them
And I look at me
And wonder: How could this ever be?

How am I, in this crazy place,
Just like the rest of the human race?

We all share a common face,
For the touch of Life can always be traced.

THE DESIGN

Somewhere along the way
Things do develop —
Progress finds a way.

We are all the toys of Time
The instrument of a planned design.
A design that can't be changed
Even if re-arranged.

In the instance of coincidence,
When the negative and positive mesh,
The design will be the same:

Inasmuch as in the realm of himself,
The creator limits the test.

BOUNCING

We bounce off
Wall after wall
And, sure enough,
No matter who it is we are,
We find our spot and place,
The ultimate trace
Of who we are.

We are the bounce
In all we do.

COMPARISON

Find the texture of the fruit

Touch the thinness of the fabric

See the light reflecting through

Measure what you feel is new.

It seems the same

What things create

And, yet, compared they cannot be,

Like the fruits that climb a tree

They are different, though the same.

There are different strings of me,

Me who is the same:

Me, the very plain.

INFINITY WILL ALWAYS BE

Live by the clock

And know you are a part of time.

Each moment must make its mark

Each experience creates a time.

YOUTH

How youth is but a giant wave

That crashes to the shore;

To let you for a moment see

The ocean that was yours.

CRYING VIOLIN

You say too well the things that mean so much.

Your voice sings of the blooming flower after

The rain that falls.

My heart is such a flower that blooms,

As Life itself.

In all your songs.

SOLANGE

The Woman

The Mother

The Example

Of the wisdom in a smile

Of the beauty in a touch

Of the love in a heart:

My Mother,

A Picture of Perfection.

EMOTIONAL CORNERSTONES

Emotional cornerstones

Live

In

The

Cross-fire

Of self-evaluation.

LISTEN

Tonight is very quiet

And so very calm is the voice

Of the quiet night that speaks to me.

Gosh, it is exciting to dream in silence.

The peaceful dream that breathes the night

Gives strength.

Problems have passed in this silence,

And love has lived its pain in silence.

This tranquil night knows it all

And I sit here . . . listening.

YOU AND THE OTHER GUY

It's you and the other guy

The other day
The other night

It's the other guy you saw being kissed good night.

How you laughed with them and could pretend

That the moon was full and the sun was bright

How the World stood still for you and the other guy

The other day
The other night

And the music plays to portray that love does stay

You've touched love's song

That never played too long into your Life

So, you sing with the other guy who

> *Owns the day*
> *And*
> *Lives the night*

It's the other guy who always seems to have it right

Is it true that songs

Were only meant for those

Who play it right,

> *Or can one believe*
>
> *The unchained melody*
>
> *That clings ever-lastingly in sight?*

THOUGHTS

The darkest night

The brightest day

The shortest moment

The longest hour

The softest touch

The deepest feeling

Reflections and

The realities of being:

> *The finger at my brow*

> *Has found a resting place.*

I AM THINKING

I am thinking

Of this moment;

This very quiet spot.

I am thinking

Tomorrow's moment

Of journeys filling thoughts.

I am thinking

How this thinking

Plants tomorrow's restless thoughts.

I am thinking

Of this thinking

That fills Life's well with thoughts.

I am thinking — always thinking

Far too many thoughts.

SPEECHLESSNESS

The lack of words to express

Often comes at a time

Of a world of understanding.

THE OLD WOMAN

The Old Woman
Was sitting,
And eating alone.

She survived the years,
And I wanted to talk to her:
The aura of her Life questioned me.

Her braided hair,
Styled with the comb of thought,
Showed the care she had given to her Life.

Her walk,
The steps of experience.

Now I too am old, and
I wish I could see her again
To touch the strength
In the wisdom of her character.

INNER STRENGTH . . .

THE EXPERIENCE BECOMES

THE INNER STRENGTH

POLKA DOTS

Polka dots

Ten thousand watts

Generally found

And lost in spots.

Feel the space

Where it all takes place.

MY VERY SPECIAL FLOWER

Suddenly, the rounded corners of your

Heart-shaped leaves have found the jagged point of

My pen; no longer can I draw your softness by a rounded

End.

Each point of you is sharp, Both to the eye

And to the touch; You see I've lived your rounded softness

Through the sharpest touch.

So from now on this flower will remind me, Never

To forget, How I've grown to draw my squiggle To be more

Perfect yet.

HERE IT WHEN YOU SEE IT

Everyone's around
On this sandy beach called existence.

Hear it when you see it
Know it when you love it
Find love when you touch it.

Be the very person
That has made you jump to see
The sounds that are around you
That change the very seas.

It's nothing but the moment
That suddenly appears
To find you in its heart
To let you feel it's near.

Love it all
With all the waves
That linger to your shore
Explore and be the one
To open up your door.

You'll feel and be alive
And God will see that you survive
And a message will be thine
For living for that time.

SO STRONG

"It seems you're so strong," He said to me;

And I,

I said,

"I have to be, because I'm too weak on the inside."

I knew I must be strong enough not to do

What I'm too weak to feel.

"YOU DON'T" AND "I MUST"

When "One Does"

    And "One Doesn't,"

"One" must do what one does,

    Until it's questioned by the other.

Hated to question you . . .

    It wasn't what I wanted to do.

I enjoyed the way it was,

    But your love didn't know

That "I must" love you.

"You Don't" and because "I Must,"

    "One" must do, as I have done

In my effort to keep things as you have done,

    For your own way, and just for you,

"I must" . . . leave you.

A PRIVILEDGED GLIMPSE

In quiet contemplation in my livingroom
Here I sit snuggling close to the firewood
Embraced by the restless burning flames.

The burning crackling wood loses itself in
The warmth of the fire and crumbles at its
Touch —

> So too my burning heart crumbles
> As my soul yearns to escape.

The world is cold and ashes remain where
Fires have been, and wood is hard to find.

Men dare not leave an ember, but want a
Glowing flame —

> Abstruse in their promiscuity.

Forever golden are the flames:
Forever darkened without aims.

I want to love, and I'm in a hurry:
But God only knows how the weather is cold.

Sparkling champagne warms my stomach.
My eyes can see the weight of its warmth
As I retire into the night.

Sweet Life I want to love you with the
Strength of my comforting fire.

Let there be light in the darkness!!!

PAIN . . .

Always seems to find
Untouched emotion
That hides behind the inner strength.

Hot dropping tears
Finding the cold cheeks of reality.

It hurts to know how Life is
Much too fragile, how easily things
Can change in the hair of a moment.

SURPRISE!

I write, I write

"How can it be?"

I didn't know

I didn't see.

I didn't know

It could not be.

I didn't know

It wasn't free.

So, now that I've found the cost,

The price was much too dear.

Seasonings of things

Beyond the price remain —

The taste of "Insight."

CONFIDENCE VERSUS RESISTANCE

Do you know the meaning of confidence?

I believed I did, when I believed in you:

> *The trust of you:*
> *To listen to*
> *And know it's true*

> *Your spoken words*
> *Would never slur*

But now resistance
Of this confident acceptance,
Of this struggle to keep what I believed was true.
What I believed of you,
Has brought me face-to-face
With the confidence of myself.

Knowing now it's not in you,
It must be in me.

You've set me free,
Which is what I never searched to be.
By knowing confidence,
You have taught me resistance.

THE NIGHT IS SILENT

Pen in hand and thoughts awake,

I find I must communicate.

Shadows of the night reflecting

The reality of the day,

Echoing the mystery of Life.

Why is it I am slowly dying in search for Life?

Will the echo of my song live its reflection

And be heard?

> *The night is silent!*

STRENGTH

Can disappointment be a strength I cannot see?

I'm afraid it will see me

Before I've had the time to look to find it there.

Scary is this place;

Scary to know nothing can be erased.

But strength is here

In the moment near.

The moment's disappointment will be the strength

In the decision of tomorrow.

TO KEEP THE FUN

It's better to know the formula

Than to swallow the solution.

Let's create,

Then leave things at their sake.

Never follow

Where stayings run

And, so, you always keep the fun.

SOME CALL IT WEAKNESS

Yes, there are many — many, many weaknesses.

But, if you stand strong to know

Where it is you find suffering in weakness,

Weakness will tempt you, but present you . . .

With a sudden choice,

    And you will find

    The way to strength.

DISAPPOINTMENT

When you get mad,

Just be glad

It's only the moment

That meets you so.

You'll escape tomorrow

To a different hour:

The sun will shine

Again you'll be fine.

Be positive.

Your thoughts of negative reaction

Expel impurity,

Accelerating concepts of organic relativity.

A DIAMOND LOST

It was a startling realization
How suddenly it was missing
From my best and special ring

But it was just a stone
That could be replaced
And the experience would be erased

And now,
To my delight,
The discomfort of the episode
Gives me a ring
That shines more light . . .

        A ring I would not have had,
        But for the loss and pain
        That left in me
        A way to start again.

I'M FINE

I'm fine,

I don't need a dime.

I live to forgive

The things that don't live.

My ego is there

To be strength to my errors.

I'm glad that I am

A woman that stands.

Sensitivity can't be canned

Or limited to any errand.

You either feel it, or you don't

And then you know the things that won't.

TRAVELING

Finding the road that leads you here

Knowing the way it's disappeared.

Then you'll note the way it's been

Is the only way it could have been.

The road is clear when it is found

And going back has made its sound.

Forward steps are hard to do

Landing marks when found are true:

Creating the creation that just had to be

The sound of the tune before the tune could see.

ANTICIPATE THE FUTURE

If only Man could have the foresight

To see his way clear through Life's impediments,

Life would be full of stepping stones creating

New paths for travel, not a faceless mirror.

Today should be a happy reflection

Of a future you anticipate.

THE STAGE

Life is an artificially lighted stage

That becomes reality in the truest sense of being —

    In the heart of the mind

For the mind looks far beyond the vision of the moment,

To the mystery of it all.

Aim for your purpose in searching for your goal,

And do not be distracted by the radiating daylight,

Or be tranquiled by the darkness in the night.

Set your own stage —

    And appreciate the visions of camoflage

    Along the way

Find your reason, and be a cause:

    And realize a visibility

    That stretches far beyond

    The pool of light surrounding.

COINS OF LUCK

Coins of luck

Are thrown

Hard and through

A solid wind.

SELF-CONTROL

Do not fall victim to your own extravagant needs!

> *"In the sweat of thy face*
> *Shalt thou eat bread"*

Bread that is yours to enjoy with the taste

Of satisfaction.

Only the mind can feed true needs:

> *Premises punched*

> *With holes of logic.*

POSITIVE THINKING

Be strong in your thoughts

And your actions will be true:

You'll know exactly what to do.

"SO NATURALLY"

"So Naturally," the tendency:

> *Solemnity finds*
> *The intercalming rhyme.*

"So Naturally," the tendency:

> *In time*
> *The ocean slowly winds.*

"So Naturally," the tendency:

> *To reach the grasping hooks.*

"So Naturally," the tendency:

> *Will leaders*
> *Find a road.*

"So Naturally," the tendency:

> *For the wind*
> *To leave a breeze.*

"So Naturally," the tendency:

> *That makes us all survive.*

FOOTSTEPS

*In every quiet corner
There sits a lonely maid.*

*She listens to the footsteps
Of the quiet parade.*

*She dare not step into the wind
To find out where she could have been.*

*The winds do blow, and people go,
But she will dream of fallen snow.*

*She finds some warmth in cold corners
And knows she cannot trust
The lust of "must."*

SING OF TODAY

Sing of today
Finding it here,
Lend me your time
And I will lend you an ear.

I sit here
To be near,
I touch you
Out of fear.

I want strength
From my weakness,
I want hope from despair.

As all things stand
On the feet of pain,
I find quiet salvation
In reaching for a name
In the hands of your understanding.

STRICTLY BUSINESS . . .

IT'S ALL SO PERFECTLY CLEAR

TO TIE THE KNOT

Tick-tock,

It's time we tied the knot.

The package has been made

And left without a name.

The value is unclaimed,

The merchandise to blame.

THE BOTTOM LINE

Some abstract thoughts

Are found to exist

While some simple yet pure beginnings

Do not persist.

Spellings are different,

The words are the same,

The bottom line

Is the name of the game.

As in "Loves Me," "Loves Me Not" —

Spellings are different,

But the words, they are the same,

As the bottom line,

That is the name of the game.

PUNCTUATION

Talk to me with punctuation!

You cleverly choose words to masticate.

Words that speak in actions

Are hard to swallow!!

HIS CONSTITUTION

For Himself

By Himself

With Himself

To Himself

"A Toughy"

AGREEMENT

If you really care,

Then you'll go —

More far away,

And let it be;

Because we can, but won't agree.

THE MARRY-ME, MARRY-ME JOKE

You must do what you must,

Thus go away together with my trust.

The rules that you apply

Seem more proper than I.

I was never wronged by you,

For it was something fun to do.

So, now that things have been spoken for,

It's time that I walk through the door

To places that we've never been

And leave you to stay where you may at your whim.

"One-Hundred Percent" is what he wants,

So let's try to understand what the man's about:

If magnetism is not what "counts,"

>*But one who rather not speaks out;*

>*Yet, a "single" percent cannot begin to grow*

>*Without the magnetism of the flow.*

So, if one is not to settle for nothing but the most,

Who'd ever think to say:

>*"One-Hundred Percent" does not make "sense."*

SARCASM

So nice to know a man
So gentle with his hands.

The frankness of his lust
Makes me wish I could throw-up.

But he's really quite a guy
For he knows just how to dive
Into the waters that await
The coming of the bait.

And then with just a little splash,
He indicates the sudden dash.

But so commanding is the man,
You must admit that he is grand.

He knows just when he can pretend
And knows just when the story ends.

He knows he was not meant to really be
Any part to a lady.
He only reaches out to them
Because they surely need a friend.

This man,
He is so good to know
For he will always be there to say "Hello."

THE PRISONER

You long to be "free"; yet, you are

Always questioning the "cost,"

A water-and-oil predicament:

For the freedom expense of "living" Life

Itself cannot be "paid" in value judgements.

"GOOD-BYE"

As soon as time goes by
The blink of an eye
Will cover the time when we were lovers.

The value of our touch will be remembered
As a single grain of sand —
Or maybe even a morning that we found in our hands.

T'was nothing but a murmur of sounds around,
A single cry without direction,
An imitation of real affection.

"Thanks" for the correction!
I appreciate your imperfections

Will no longer be looking in your direction

Carry on, My Paragon:

May you live long and prosper
And never know the taste of lobster.

Should our shadows ever cross
In elevators that are lost,
Do not bother to say "Hello"
For I will understand that you must go.

I DON'T WANT YOU

I don't want you
It's much easier to kiss
And say Good-Bye
It's not meant to be
What we ought to be
You are wrong for me
Good-Bye.

I don't want you
It's much easier to kiss
And say Good-Bye
The days we'll miss
Forget the bliss
So, Good-Bye
Let it die
Good-Bye.

Good-Bye, My Love
Good-Bye, My Need
No time to lose
I am far from you
Never wanted you
But I needed you

It's much easier to forget
Away from you, My Pet
So, Good-Bye, as we die
Let it lie.

I don't want you
It's much easier to kiss
And say Good-Bye.
Now you see we cannot be
Never you, never me

So, kiss the sky
Let us fly
Say Good-Bye

Just say Good-Bye
As I sigh
Good-Bye
To a high
Good-Bye
To the moon
Good-Bye
Life's Balloon

Good-Bye!

T'IS THE SEASON

T'is the season
For Life to begin
T'is the season
To find a reason.

Life always seemed to be
What was waiting for me:
But it's too long a wait,
The dates have become fate.

I see.
I disagree.
Life's haunting me.

I'm going to live it now,
Feet on the ground . . .

       Try to make the best
       Of the efforts that stand ahead.

Write me the reason,
I'll find you the season.

No more "Whys" would be a lie,
But I'll survive to know the time of the season . . .

       Hold Me!

NATURE . . .

SPEAKS OF "TIME,"

AND "TIME" IS ALL WE HAVE

YESTERDAY'S SUNSET

Yesterday's sunset

Is the beginning of today.

THE FUNDAMENTAL WIND

The howling wind
Sounds steps of time:

Missles of emotion

I love this wind
Where freedom dares to feel
In gasping breaths of
Occupied expression

We walk against the wind,
Though scary when it blows,
We survive the wind, you know

The fundamental wind
Remembers the ingredients
That spill into our Life
As the howling wind tonight.

THE SUN

The Sun and Earth in the morning
  Kiss each other in a cold and unsuspecting night

  As its rays of warmth awaken
  To cast a piercing touch
  Upon the shadows of the Earth

And beauty flowers
  Beyond the words of any Man
  To captivate the spirit
  As it blankets the Earth.

THE OCEAN

To hear the roaring tides
And live the passion in its wind.

To breathe and taste its salty kiss
And lose yourself in all its mist

To bring you so close
And yet be so far
From knowing who you really are.

THE BIRDS

Birds have the freedom of soaring the sky
Leaving Man to only visualize
The path that he would emulate
The path his heart and soul would take.

Above the trees
About the clouds
To harmonize with Nature's moods
To feel her love, the sun
Her restlessness the wind

To wrestle with Nature in weathering the storm
In the search of the peace and warmth to follow

To "Live" the meaning of Nature's way.
To reach the heights that one can soar,
Without forgetting where you are.

FLYING . . . WITH THE MUSIC OF THE SKY

The Stradivarius of the sky
Sings out rainbows found in time . . .
A redish streak against the blue.
Shines the time from me to you.

Time does sing the moment's glow
That leads to shimmering rainbows.

Time does streak as colors flow
And little-by-little Life lets go.

Night finds the light of day
Rhyming ways light interplays:

>*Rivers of night*
>*Streams of light*
>*Blue on blue, the day on night*

The shimmering sun piercing through rooted hues
Landing now, as we descend
Time winds slower, as it ends.

And colors remain to speak again
In the memory of a song
That never really ends.

THE MARVEL OF THINGS

Winter falls from the trees,
So pretty are melting leaves.

Each season's touch yearns for its
Moment of expression.

As if never before seen,
        Each picture of Life is gleaned
        Into the marvel of things:

It's new again,
Reborn again

A time again,
A long lost friend

To know again . . .

        An absent wind
        A warm blue sky,
        The wind that dies

        The sound of rain
        The distant train
        That hot hello
        That takes you home
        To quiet days
        In wooded trees.

NATURE'S OWN

The empty tree

Whose leaves have left

Sets a picture of the tree

As an extension of the surrounding ground.

And so is Man,

When left alone,

An extension of himself

As Nature's Own.

THE FLOWER

For every little flower

There is a bud that blooms.

There is the rain that falls

In pursuit of roots.

And so is Man

A flower or a bud

And when not nourished, a dud.

VOICES . . .

MY EARS ARE THE VESSELS

OF AN ETCHED HEART,

THAT STRUGGLES TO FIND

THE WAY

THE TRINITY

Take it where you see it to be
It's there for you if you look to see
There's the trinity in things that be
There's true ecstasy in syncope.

Join with the light, begin to unwind
See where you go, as you learn what you know

Through the you in the day
Through the night on the way
There are the thoughts that do stay.

's the words that we talk
Through the doors of hard knocks

There's the days in our lives
That the years do survive

There's so much in a crack
That the egg starts to hatch

There's the joy in the dream
That is yet unforeseen

There's the power of insight
That begins to take flight

There's the arrow of connection
That drives in the reflection

Many acts of discipline
Drive it home
To where it is you've been

It's latching on to you,
The ways that seemed brand new

But the fish are in the pond
And the water's never gone
And suddenly the swans
Swim along to set the dawn.

THE CHILD

The call of the wild will always be heard

   First by the child

He listens more to know

   How quietly things grow.

Before the sounds that grownups hear

   When loud enough to reach their ear,

The child sees more than we can see

   For he anticipates any mystery.

We all become a little deaf

   As we all believe that we progress

   Mysteries here, and quiet there

   Just makes us know we do not care.

Sensitivity becomes rare

   As senility finds the chair.

THE ONENESS OF MAN

All Men are one.

As a university of science

We inter-relate because

We are one mass of logic,

Essentially the way of Man.

We live the science of life and emotion

In petrified steps of time.

Time seals The Oneness of Man

To sound in common levels of frequency called sound.

The components of sound

Invent physics in scientific minds

As energies combine to invent chemistry.

Man, with his surroundings,

Is hurled so fast

That things appear beyond their grasp.

PAGES OF PEOPLE

People are as papers are,

Speaking imprisoned themes

In quiet reflection of

Contemplated thoughts.

Faces forming sounds,

Views of thought:

    Semblance of voice

    Semblance of mind

    Semblance of a city in transit.

I'M HIDING

Yes, I'm hiding
Hiding from the people
Who want to know me for reasons.

Why should I let them touch
A real part of me, when, really,
They care not beyond a reason,
And only want to share through curiosity.

So, I hide in places that I know . . .
Belong to me,
Where I can be free to play and say:

> "It's only me and who I am today"
> "I love in my way,"
> And
> "It matters not how profits sway"

I love the quiet in the day
And those who look to see me there,
Find a friend.

THE LOVERS' KISS

As lovers kiss and the ocean's waves crash,

Climbing far beyond the sand —

Life goes by in quiet sounds.

PEARLS

No more poetry to write,

For words are few

When all the music and all the pearls

In the ocean lie "suddenly" as whispering thoughts.

I hear them as I see them

In images so blue

As glances form so many points of view.

"I'M ONLY TALKING"

Oh, "I'm only talking."

But on the inside, I feel that I'm yelling.

I often stop myself and wonder:

> *"Am I speaking too loudly?"*

I have this churning desire to yell

The feelings I can't dispel.

SILENCE

I love the silence in this room,

For it embraces me

And lets the borders of my mind expand into

The strength of its walls.

Face-to-face we share the light

As we look into the darkness of the future

    And the dimness of the past —

And the moment as it resounds in echos

Of peace and objectivity.

SYMPHONY

Love and the ocean
Love and the wind

Together forever:
The ocean and the wind

The eyes of the night
The colors of the day
Are reflected in the beats of my heart
As I listen to the harmony in the music it plays.

Its rhythm fills my soul,
My thoughts,
My every movement.

It speaks of the seriousness of Life
It echos moods and feelings of many traveled roads.

JOGGING

Everything is calm

As we run along.

We are the ones who make the sounds

For all we see around.

I'M AT PEACE

I'm at peace
With the child in me
Whose wrinkled pictures
Mark my questing heart.

Can a word
Be the peace
Of a thousand desperate moments?

I'm so strong
With silent words this day.
Never used to find the words to say.

It could be I'm getting older.
I'm happier today —
    Accepting, accepting . . . accepting . . .

       Thoughts about tomorrow
       That may or may not flower

In the distant hour
Cozily tucked away . . .
Another day.

THE OUNCE

It is the ounce of investment
Which covers a distance of an inch in size

It is a unit of measure
Of an approximate outgoing thumb
Which leads you toward direction

An ounce of time
Such a small measure
Of such a precise distance
Which leads to enormous growth

As in an ounce of love
Or an ounce of perfection

And how can one explain in depth the perception?

It is a small shadow
Of a perfect larger thing

The ounce captures it all
Within a rubber string
That molds the inches to join itself
Into congestion
That won't let go

So, when a unit ounce measures up
Into a picture of perfection
It is the ounce of predilection
The kiss of detection
The rumor of suggestion
The ounce.

SUNDAY

I have an order

    For a hug and a squeeze

And it's in the breeze

    That I feel today.

I'm in the breeze of love,

    And

It is here that I survive as Woman.

"CONGRATULATIONS"

"Congratulations" are the wings of Success!

WINDOW CROSSINGS...

ROADS OF PERPENDICULAR ATTRACTION:

CROSS-WORD PUZZLES FILLING IN

LINES OF TIME

WINDOW CROSSINGS

People crossing each other
As a roadmap crosses roads of perpendicular attraction.

"Realism" — Realizing it's been there
    In a point of Time.

Cross-word puzzles filling in lines of Time.

Can it be we peer through window crossings that meet,
And meet again . . .

    To view beyond what longs to be your friend.

YESTERDAY

It seemed only yesterday

A child dreamed

What her Life would be.

Dreams of yesterday

Find the reality of today . . .

The reality of today

Still knows the dream of yesterday.

Yesterday,

I'll see you today

Yesterday,

Never goes away.

GROWTH

Finally it's more

It could not be less.

It grew from lesser things, it seems.

And so the lesser things have streamed

To the epitomy of the most:

The lesser things create The Host.

MOMENTS GRAY

Quiet night
Forgetting light

The new found day
That slips away

Moments gray
That never stay

Finding words
That I have learned

Touching thoughts
That were hard earned.

Here and there,
I find a curve:
Around the bend
There is no end

Headlines find what time has meant
Right and wrong
Stretching along.

In quiet nights
Forgetting lights
Progressing time shall bring new light.

DESTINY TIES VERSATILITY

I do believe in a destiny . . .

A destiny for all

The glass and diamonds of the Earth.

"We" are the elements . . . "We" are

The quality in refinement
The elements in the crude:

A bed of sand
In our homeland . . .

So versatile we think we are,

In such a tightly packed jar.

LIFE . . .

Is a cubicle of space.

As in one day at a time,
It is a movement of the hand
Deciding air and land.

Life is hard to know
Until some choice is made
And then you can't avoid
The references employed.

IT'S REALLY HAPPENING

Life goes by so fast
It's hard to write everything down.

The days lose themselves in years,
Time seems to disappear.

THINK ABOUT IT

The moment's time

Is more temporary

Than the moment's effort.

ALLOW ME TO ELUCIDATE

"Well"?

And "So"?

"If"?

And "No."

"Yes,"

And "When"?

The View:

And "Then"?

Momentum bends:

The "Well,"

The "So,"

The "If,"

The "No,"

The "Yes," and "When,"

The "Then,"

The Story Ends.

"JUST THE SAME"

Just The Same

I'll always be

Viewing from the balcony . . .

Life's embrace and constant stare.

Between images

Are unfinished truths:

Images we faced and pulled away from . . .

"Just The Same"

Disconnected to explode in reality's circuit,
As we view things anew . . .

"Just The Same."

REALIZATION

Another step closer to myself and the realizations

Of the fire and emotion that live in me.

Life seems more real than ever

As every perception speaks out louder than before,

And calmness permeates beauty as it speaks.

The logistics of the mathematical equation of Life

Are divided into its equal parts:

> *I weigh now the moment*
> *And see in the future*
> *How soon it will be a link to the past*

To be able to hold a future as we touch the moment!

Each moment is the future, and each moment must be

Remembered and kept.

THAT SOLITARY STAR

Realities are composed beginnings

Disciplined to talk by the essence

Of their shining light.

A light reflecting

In the mirror of thine eyes.

No matter where you are,

That solitary star always shines . . .

That solitary star is You.

DEATH

The drama of Life is real.

Simple decisions begin reactions

Which open hours that reflect to create the moment.

The moment races into an expanding future,

Influencing the totality of each individual's canvas;

A masterpiece created to merge with the totality of

Remission that meets the beginning of other diversities.

Death releases the canvas to remain and symbolize

The strokes of Time

    As the creator escapes

    To live again as never before.

THE PASSENGER

From the window, I see Life go by.

How quick the shutter of the camera closes

To take a picture of Life to remember;

And, yet, how many people will still

Close their eyes to the picture? . . .

> *They get something in their eye,*
>
> *And feel it in their chest.*

They're busy rushing down their tracks,

They dare not look back . . .

> *They leave their feelings*
>
> *Far behind!*

PATIENCE

Patience must be had
So the wind can blow
And the ship can sail

Patience must be had
To allow for the lightning path

Patience need only appear
When you know something is near
And you can't believe your ears

Patience, My Friend,
Will bless you in the end
If only you could cheer, not before,
But when the time is here for what you want so dear.

So, grant me patience, My Dear God, But . . . "HURRY"!

THE END AND THE BEGINNING

The End And The Beginning

> *Have met someplace along the way*

Who's to know where quiet waters begin to flow

> *And where they suddenly must End.*

ALPHABETICAL INDEX OF POEMS

NOTES

NOTES

NOTES

NOTES

NOTES

NOTES